Confidence in God

*W*ORDS OF ENCOURAGEMENT
*taken from the Notes, Instructions and
Letters of Rev. Daniel Considine, S. J.
Arranged by Rev. F. C. Devas, S. J.*

THE SIGN ✝ MAGAZINE
MONASTERY PLACE
UNION CITY, NEW JERSEY

FOREWORD

THESE Words of Encouragement, reprinted by permission of the Catholic Truth Society of London, are selections made from Father Considine's notes, instructions and letters.

Father Considine's manner was marked by simplicity and directness: if he had a platitude to repeat, he did not attempt to disguise it in fine language; nor did he hesitate to stress a particular truth with an apparent disregard for other truths, which to the casual reader may prove disconcerting. Thus it would be difficult to discover in a textbook of theology the equivalent of the statement, "God is shy": while the lukewarm and frivolous might easily take false comfort when reading that "to resign myself to a distraction for God's sake is union with God."

The practical needs of the honest, but puzzled, individual were the object of Father Considine's solicitude; such individuals will find in his printed words what others found in them when they were spoken—encouragement and enlightenment.

Imprimatur: ✠THOMAS J. TOOLEN, D.D.
Bishop of Mobile

Confidence in God

"But he that had received the one talent came
and said. Lord, I know that Thou art a hard
man."—Matt. xxv. 24.

IF we don't look upon God as a hard
man we have every reason to con-
gratulate ourselves. We say we think Him
merciful, kind, loving, but in our hearts we
look upon Him as hard. Three-quarters of
the troubles of good people come from this.
He feels intensely our misconception of
Him. We look upon Him as a hard
grasping man, who wants to get all He
can out of us and give nothing in return.
And woe betide us if we fail to satisfy
Him. This is utterly wrong.

If God has ever shown me any love He
must love me still. God does not care for
me one day and hate me the next. He is
not capricious or inconstant like man.
Above everything, God wants my love,

3

and with love come happiness and enthusiasm in His service. We think: I have
only one talent; others have five. Therefore I will do nothing but bury mine. I
will run no risks. But each of our tem-
peraments and characters has been fitted
exactly, thought out from all time to suit
our lives. What others have would not
suit me. What we have we don't value;
what we have not we desire. Do not say,
God evidently, from my capabilities, does
not care much for me; does not expect
much from me. God craves your love.
Ask, ask, ask for graces and you will
assuredly get them.

✠   WATCH THE PRESENT   ✠

DO not cry over spilt milk. Do not
dwell on the faults and sins of the
past. Leave them alone; leave them to
God. As soon as possible make an Act
of Contrition and never think of them
again. Often the despondence caused by
sin is more wrong, and keeps one away
from God more than the sin itself. Don't
waste time being discouraged. Get up and
go to God. Draw near to Him. Do not
stand back hanging your head.
  Do what thou doest. Some people always have one eye on the past and the

other on the future, instead of both on the
present. Don't waste time deploring the
past and being apprehensive of the future.
Grace will be given to meet each day the
difficulties of that day. There are very
few people who would not be good at their
own job if they would only develop the
power of concentration. It is this incessant worrying over past and future that
prevents the concentration. Leave the
future in God's hands.

✠   **THINK WELL OF GOD**   ✠

THINK of God in goodness. Have a
good opinion of God. God loves us to
think well of Him, to trust Him, to think
lovingly of Him. Do not think God does
not forgive easily. The more intimate a
human friendship the less nervous one is
of a chance word offending one's friend.
Friends are not lost for ever by some little
word or act displeasing them. Above all,
remember that in darkness, gloom, dejec-
tion, or depression God does not dwell.
Do not even make acts of sorrow, if that
depresses; make acts of hope and love.
Depression never comes from God; neither
does any thought which makes His service
difficult. Have always the highest opinion
of our Lord and Master.

✠   **LIFE A WARFARE**   ✠

JOB says the life of man upon earth is a continual warfare, conflict. No matter how far we are advanced in the spiritual life, we must never expect immunity from temptation; from ups and downs. St. Paul in his first Epistle to the Corinthians says, "Everyone runs, but not everyone gets a prize. Everyone that striveth for the mastery must refrain himself from many things." St. Paul is addressing people who live on the Isthmus of Corinth, a place famous at that time for beauty, art, luxury and, consequent on the latter, profligacy. But also a spot rendered famous by the games which took place there. For this reason St. Paul likens the spiritual life to games, to a race. He is not addressing those who sit under an awning watching and gently applauding the efforts of the athletes. He speaks to those who take part in the race. It is an image of the spiritual life, which entails effort, exertion, and often exhaustion.

Our Lord says: Work out your salvation; traffic until I come. He wants effort, untiring effort. The Curé d'Ars used to say when people spoke of his holiness, "I'm not afraid of trouble, that is all." Not meaning trouble in the sense of sorrow, but in the sense of labor, fatigue. We are dreadfully afraid of trouble; otherwise we should be much nearer to our Lord than we are. Man is by nature an extremely lazy animal, who likes nothing so much as to do nothing. I do not mean in a physical sense. Sometimes in a sermon or a book we hear or see something we think exactly fits ourselves. We make a resolutiton to carry it out, which we do until it costs us something. We resolve to cultivate recollection, which we do until we hear some really spicy bit of scandal, then the recollection is thrown to the winds. I should ask myself from month to month what good are these instructions doing me? If I feel tired and battered, that is no reason for dissatisfaction.

✠ WORK CUT OUT ✠

A SOLDIER in a campaign is not astonished if he is wounded or overdone from fatigue. Neither must I say in my sphere of life there is no work open to me. There is always work. If I have a bad temper there is plenty of work cut out for me for years to come. If we have that dangerous gift of saying smart things, when even our best friends have the bene-

fit of our wit at their expense, that is a
thing to fight against. I should fight like
a true soldier—full of courage, full of high
hopes. Finally, do not be astonished if
there are storms, if there is opposition, if
friends say, "Why, what has come to So-
and-so? He is becoming a perfect nuisance
with his piety. Why this fervor all of a
sudden?" For in a seemingly monotonous,
uneventful, unsuccessful life, there may
be more peace, joy, and true happiness
than in that of a person who is surrounded
with every luxury, every satisfaction, and
the love and admiration of everyone with
whom he comes in contact.

✠   BEAR WITH YOURSELF   ✠

S T. PAUL says: "I will chastise my
body and bring it into subjection, lest,
having preached to others, I myself become
a cast-away.' It is a great mistake to think
that without bodily austerities we cannot
draw very near to God. Without bodily
austerities we can withdraw all obstacles
between Himself and ourselves; we can
get a very intimate knowledge of Him and
can please Him very much. He will not
keep His choicest gifts from us because of
the way in which we are circumstanced. In
the days of great austerities nerves did not

exist. They are a product of our times. Nerves are the austerities we have to bear to-day. *Bear with yourself,* your depression, gloom, moods, variability of temper. To bear with one's self is an act of great virtue. A very great deal of evil comes from the fact that a fit of nerves is so often mistaken for something wrong with the soul.

✠   NERVOUS DEPRESSION   ✠

TO use an expression common among boys nowadays, and, unfortunately, also among the other sex — we feel rotten. Not to lose patience with ourselves when we feel rotten is a very high virtue. The worst form of nerves is depression. People really believe that they have lost faith, hope, love, everything. It is a very great trial. St. Teresa says: "The worst of sickness is that it so often weakens you, you cannot fix your thoughts on God." But this is of no consequence. It is the doing for God that is important, not the thinking of God. It is a very great trial to many of us to be unable to get everyday to Holy Communion. But to bear quietly with our weakness, because it is His will, pleases Him a great deal more than the most fervent Communion we ever made.

Headaches are a great trial. We cannot pray with a "headache." But if we bear with ourselves it is more meritorious than the best of prayers.

Bear with others. We most of us have a great deal to bear from others. It is often the reflex of what *they* have to bear from us, but still, none the less, very hard. The people we live with are not omniscient. They may be excellent, and have the best intentions, but they make mistakes; they may form hard judgments. Let us ask God to give us patience to bear with ourselves and to bear with others.

✠   HOLDING GOD'S HAND   ✠

WE ought to go through life holding God's hand. There is much suffering that has to be gone through in this life, and it makes all the difference of pleasure or pain whether we have our hand in God's or not. It will make a joy of even mortification. The Angel Gabriel said to our Lady, The Lord is with thee. We ought to make the intention every time we say the Hail, Mary of asking our Lord to be with us. Try and love God. He wants us all to be saints. It is our own fault if we are not. In spite of darkness and despondency we must keep on

asking Him to be with us. The troubles
I have are the troubles He had. For instance, monotony. He was year after
year a common carpenter; not even a
joiner. Everything He did He did in the
hope that we should imitate Him.

✠   YOUR OWN GOOD   ✠

BEAR the burden of life cheerfully,
and we are half-way to being saints.
If God treats us in the way that He treated Mary and her Son we should be only
too pleased. Health, money, success are
not His best gifts. He rarely gives them
to His dearest friends. We say, I should
like to be settled in life; have more money,
beauty, talents. Are you certain they
would be good for you? If so, He would
certainly give them to you. Our Lord is
always wondering how He can best help
us to love Him. If you find life difficult,
tell Him so; hard to be good, tell Him so.
You are suffering, or at any rate you
cannot pray — you regret it — tell God
so, that is prayer. If you try to do these
things of your own strength you will never
succeed. If you go through life holding
His hand, love will make everything easy.
"Forthwith Jesus obliged His disciples
to go up into the boat, and to go before

Him over the water." (Matt. xiv. 22.)   A voyage thus begun we should have thought would be most prosperous, undertaken by a direct command of our Lord Himself. The Disciples embarked and began their journey in order to do the Will of God. Surely it will be a most favorable one!

On the contrary, they met an adverse wind, rough seas, and everything that was difficult.   "But the boat in the midst of the sea was tossed with the waves: for the wind was contrary." (Matt. xiv. 24.) The sea raged, the wind howled, the little boat was tossed about — and Jesus was not there!   Our Lord was with them, but it was His Will they should have this difficulty.   It is necessary to meet many troubles in His service, even when we are most truly doing His Will.

✠   BE OF GOOD HEART   ✠

OUR Lord allowed these tribulations to befall His Disciples to show His watchful love over them.   He allows troubles to befall us in order to make us long for Him, think of Him, turn to Him, trust in Him, and call upon Him for help.

Far from losing courage, we ought to redouble our efforts in His service and work fearlessly, however loudly the winds and the waves may roar. He sees and knows all, and awaits His own time. In His own time He will come, even walking on the waters of tribulation.

"And in the fourth watch of the night He came to them, walking upon the sea. And they seeing Him were troubled, and they cried out for fear. And immediately Jesus spoke to them, saying: 'Be of good heart: it is I, fear ye not.'" (Matt. xiv. 25-27.) Often in trouble we cry out, and He answers in our hearts. He often comes to us in that very tribulation which hides Him from us saying: "Be of good heart: it is I, fear not."

✠   LOOKING TO JESUS   ✠

PETER, full of impetuous love, hearing the voice of his Master, cries out, "If it be Thou bid me come to Thee upon the waters." (Matt. xiv. 28.) Bid me come to Thee! And He said, "Come!" Then Peter walked upon the water to come to Jesus. Fervent love offers itself for any service, believes nothing impossible, is ready for all.

St. Peter walks happily towards Jesus as long as he looks at Him alone, but the moment he looks at the waves and himself he sinks. Look at Jesus, not at self or at

danger. Then St. Peter cried out: "Lord,
save me!" And immediately Jesus stretch-
ed out His hand, took hold of him, and
said, "Oh, thou of little faith, why didst
thou doubt?" Jesus and Peter entered the
boat. And the wind ceased; calm reigned
around. Then they adored Jesus, saying:
"Indeed. Thou art the Son of God."

☩   IN HIS KEEPING   ☩

"MY lots are in Thy hands." (Ps. xxx.
15.) Suppose, my God, You had
told us that, as we know the value of our
soul, You were going to trust us with the
choice of the means by which its salvation
is to be worked out; You were going to put
before us riches and poverty, sickness and
health, success and failure, a long life and
a short one, and we might take that which
seemed best for us. Should we be content? Should we not say, if we were wise:
"My God, do not trust this to me   I shall
choose, I know I shall, what I like, not
what is best for me."

And suppose You were to tell us there
were souls to whom You would not en-
trust such a decision. Either they were
too weak, or You were so anxious to save
them that You had left the choice of means
not to themselves but to those who love

them better than they love themselves, and who would choose for them more wisely. To their Guardian Angel, to their Patron Saint, even to the Seat of Wisdom herself; and if we wished You would let us be one of those favored souls. Should we be content, then? Or should we say: "My God, forgive me for being mistrustful still. I know my Guardian Angel and my holy Patrons and, most of all, my Mother Mary, love me dearly and would do their best for me; but their wisdom after all is not infinite. They might make a mistake, and that mistake might mean the loss of everything to me. I cannot afford any risks here. My soul is my only one; I must save it whatever happens. I dare not keep it in my own hands, and I dare not trust it even to the highest and holiest and wisest of those around Thy throne."

✠   ONLY A FEW?   ✠

SUPPOSE You were to say to us: "There are a few, a very few, whose salvation is so dear to Me that I will trust the choice of means to no one. I will plan and arrange all Myself. Nothing shall happen to them but what has been foreseen and prepared from all eternity by My infinite Wisdom and Goodness. No one shall touch them, no joy or sorrow shall come in their way, no, nor a hair of their head fall to the ground without My knowledge and permission." Should we not cry out: "My God, I hardly dare ask it, but oh that I might be one of that happy chosen few, for surely they are safe!"

✠   PRIVILEGED   ✠

YOU check me by a warning: "These souls will not have their own way in life. Their road will sometimes be hard and rugged. They will see things prosper in the hands of others and fail in theirs. They will be harshly used by those around them — misjudged, set aside, unjustly treated; life to many of them will be uphill work." Do I draw back now, or do I cry out again: "No matter that, no matter that at all! What will they care when they know Your arm is around them as they go uphill; Your hand sends the cross, and the failure, and the pain! No, my God, that does not frighten me. Let me be only one of those whose lot is altogether in Your hands, and I will fear nothing; nay, I will be grateful for all that comes to me. I will kiss Your hand even when You strike me. I shall feel peaceful

and happy always in the thought that it
is the wisdom of my God that orders all
for me, and the love of my Heavenly
Father that provides everything to help
me. Let me be one of those chosen ones,
and You will see how I value my privilege,
how I prize whatever You send."

Suppose—I have been saying. But this
is no supposition. I *am* that privileged one
whose life in its minutest details is Your
ordering and Your care. How can I com-
plain, my God? How can I be mistrustful
or even anxious? "My lots are in Thy
hands."

✠   THE SACRED HEART   ✠

THE great object of the devotion to the
Sacred Heart is to teach us to love
our Lord because He loves us. We
were brought into the world solely because
He loved us, and He wanted our love. He
wants to do us good. He longs to do us
good. He wants to know us, and wants
us to know Him. He longs to heap His
love upon us, to draw us very near to Him.
We tie His hands by our coldness, our
callousness, our indifference. We have
such a wrong idea of Him. He is not
always on the look out to catch us trip-
ping; or wanting to keep us persistently **in**

suspense as to whether we shall save our souls or lose them.

"Do I love God?" you are probably thinking. "Of course I love God, but in a common-sense, practical way. I must not be carried away by hysterical excesses. Religion must fill a certain part of my life but no more. If I let myself go there is no knowing where it might end. I shall finish by finding myself in a convent or some other equally unpleasant place." This is the view of the common-sense Catholic. Am I a common-sense Catholic or an enthusiastic Catholic?

✠   FIRST THINGS FIRST   ✠

FROM our childhood many of us have been told more of the punishments God has in store for us if we fail to please Him than of the rewards He looks forward to giving when we do please Him. In preparing for Confession we spend nine minutes in examining our conscience and one minute in telling our Lord we are sorry. The first thing necessary in loving our Lord is to believe Him lovable. What are the sort of persons one loves? First, they must be easy to get on with. How many in their heart of hearts think our Lord easy to get on with? We think Him touchy, unapproachable, easily annoyed or offended. And yet all this fear of Him pains Him very much. Would our father wish us to hang our heads, be shy and shrinking in his presence? How much less so our Heavenly Father? He has an almost foolish love for us.

✠ MULTIPLIED GIFTS ✠

NEVER was a mother so blind to the faults of her child as our Lord is to ours. He makes allowances to an almost extravagant degree. He is infinitely quicker to pity and help than to blame and punish. Whatever attracts you in your fellow-creatures in His gift, and possessed by Him in a higher sense. And yet how many ascribe to Him mean and petty ways, trying to catch us, to be ungenerous — conduct we would not tolerate in human friendship. There is nothing easier than to love God, because there is nothing un-loveable in Him. God is Love. He asks our love in return. Oh, my God, do Thou fill my heart, my soul, my whole being with the fire of Thy Divine Love. Thou, my God, art the God of my heart, and my portion for ever.

There seems to be a general persuasion that God is difficult to please; that He is hard, severe, unfair. Some have too much money; others live in a state of poverty. This is unfair, so I shall not try to please Him. The poor cannot have sumptuous suppers, neither can they have *pâté de foie gras* for lunch. But this is not the fault of our Heavenly Father. Squalor, poverty, and degradation are the result of sin. The real pleasures of life are open to all: love, social life in the different spheres of society, enjoyment of nature, mountains, trees, flowers, good health.

✠   **BEGIN NOW**   ✠

WE all have a millstone hanging about our necks. We say: "The service of God is not meant for me: for others, yes; but not for me. My past or my present prevents me from ever doing anything for God. I have felt that I was meant for something good, but I did not take the opportunity. Now it is useless; I shall never do anything." Is it true that we can do nothing for God because we have not done so from the cradle? At the present moment you have a desire to please and love God. From whom does that desire come? We can't have a desire to love God unless He gives us that desire. Would God encourage us along a path which ended with "No Thoroughfare"? We do not see that cool wind which fans our cheeks, and yet we feel the movement in the atmosphere.

Thus it is with grace. In one moment He can transform the most abandoned heart into one full of love for Him. Some say: "I don't feel that God wants me to love Him; He doesn't care whether I love Him or not." Our Lord died for each one of us. Could He do more? He longs for our personal love. *High sanctity* is within the reach of *everyone*. Our Lord does not look for beauty, position, money, intellect. All He asks is correspondence to His grace. That, and that alone, is all that is necessary to become a saint.

☩ JOY VS. SADNESS ☩

WE should all do more for God if we endeavored to bring more enjoyment into our lives and into the lives of others. If the world were much better it would be much happier. St. Paul says, "Rejoice in the Lord always, and again I say rejoice." Happiness always leads to and never away from God. If we are inclined to be superior and look down on mirth and joy, there is something very wrong with our view of the spiritual life. We also do infinite harm to

religion. The world looks upon piety as
in some way connected with sadness. As
laughter is good for the body, so is cheerfulness good for the soul.

People will say, "We are not told that
our Lord ever laughed." On the other
hand, we are told that our Lord was loved
wherever He went. And who is so little
loved as a wet-blanket, who carries a
ramping atmosphere of gloom and depression wherever she goes. It is no sign of
sanctity to fail to find pleasure and amuse-
ment in what pleases and amuses others.
Let us make our own service of God as
easy as possible. It is our Lord Himself
Who has said, "My yoke is sweet and My
burden light. Come to Me, and I will refresh you."

✠   TAKE TIME   ✠

ONE of the greatest mistakes in the
spiritual life is a lack of preparation. We are all in such a hurry to be
better, to be holy. Half the secret of success in teaching consists in repetition, yet
no one wants to repeat. No one likes the
grind of the grammar. In our spiritual life
we want to skip declensions, genders,
verbs, and syntax. We want to get into
close relationship with God. We expect

to pray with no distractions. We want
to read God's secrets before we can spell.
God's friends are, above all, humble; we
want grounding, we want spade-work.

We don't prepare ourselves for the in-
spirations of the Holy Spirit. We wonder,
after the way we have tried, that we are
not better. Very different from the saints,
who are always thanking God that they
are not worse. If you really are going forward you probably think you are going
backward. If you open the door of a dark
room you cannot see the dust or dirt that
is in it. But if you open even a chink of
the shutter, then it is that you see the
dust. The more light you let in the more
dust you notice. Thus it is with God's
light. The more do we ask the Holy
Ghost to pour His illuminating light into
our souls, the more do we notice our
faults.

✠   AXE TO THE ROOT   ✠

IN the old days you had no faults
Everyone else had lots. "So-and-so is
so selfish," "so bumptious," "so uncharitable." The better you become the more
good you see in others. God did not think
four thousand years too long a time in
which to prepare the world for the coming

of His Son. St. John the Baptist says,
"The axe is put to the root." Let us put the
axe to the root of those faults which keep
us from our Lord. It is not the reading of
pious books, or the saying of long prayers, or science, or knowledge, which intro-
duces the Child Jesus into our hearts. It
is the love, it is the longing for Him to be
there, that brings Him. It is the real effort that it costs us to put the axe to the
root. We know what He loves, we know
what He dislikes. If you want Him you
must not be afraid to pay the price. Let
us ask our Lord what faults we are to try
to get rid of by way of preparation to re-
ceiving Him into our hearts.

✠   PERSONAL QUESTIONS   ✠

AM I using to the full the grace of God?
Have I reason for supposing that God
wants me to lead a better life than hitherto? Does He want to come into my heart?
Is it not a little presumptuous, rather emo-
tional, to think that our Lord really wants
to make my heart His own? In order to
make no one nervous, I will say at once
that in speaking of God's calls I do not
mean in any sense a call to religious life.
The feeling of unrest, of spiritual dissatisfaction; the feeling that I've not really got

hold of the one thing which can fill my life; the sensation of the emptiness, hollowness of the world: these feelings do not come from myself, still less do they come from the Devil.

✠   CALLS FROM GOD   ✠

WHY should we stir up still waters? They are calls from God. If these thoughts take shape in my mind it is a certain indication that God wants me to draw nearer to Him, to do better. Our Lord has different ways of calling different people. St. Andrew and St. John were walking with St. John the Baptist, who said, "Behold the Lamb of God." Sts. John and Andrew followed after our Lord and asked Him where He was lodging. Our Lord said, "Come and see." They went with Him, stayed all night, and next morning said, "Now we have found the Messiah." St. Peter was called while mending his nets. The rich young man said, "Good Master, what must I do to possess eternal life?" "Keep the commandments." "I do so." Our Lord looked at him and loved him. "Then if thou wouldst be *perfect*, go sell all thou hast and give to the poor, and come follow Me?"

OUR Lord calls us in different ways. I am not speaking of a religious vocation, but a call to lead a better life. Our Lord says, "I want you to become a special friend of mine; to break with whatever you know to be unworthy of you. I want you to be perfect, to be willing to sell all you have to follow Me." I am not speaking of selling all in a literal sense. Our Lord says, "If you want to be perfect you must let *nothing* stand between you and Me; there must be nothing held back: no deliberate affection for anything opposed to My Will." The standard is high, but our Lord's words are, "If thou wouldst be perfect." Are there things in my heart which pull me away from our Lord? What has been stopping me from real peace of soul? Am I too fond of admiration? Do I set too much store on the affection of others? Some of us hear the voice of God loud enough to make us uncomfortable and still we won't give in. Is there anything I am holding back? Am I quite happy? Quite satisfied? He asks: "Are you willing to give Me anything I want? To do whatever I ask of you? *Come follow Me.*" This is Christ's command addressed to each of us.

He Who made our hearts knows how to attract them. Misery is the element of Satan. Joy is the element of our Lord. The highest joy is to be found in His service. He wants us to be near Him, because to be near Him is happiness. He wants us to be like Him, because to be like Him is happiness. He wants us to become less selfish; to think more of others, more of Him; to love Him and to help others to love Him. Is He not worth following? Beg of Him to make His call so clear as to be unmistakable, and have the generosity to be content, and even anxious, to follow whithersoever He may lead.

✠   ASK WITH SINCERITY   ✠

WE all make mistakes. What we ought to do is to profit by them. How am I to find out what God wants me to do? St. Paul said: "Lord, what wouldst Thou have me do?" If we say this from our hearts our Lord *never* refuses an answer. Some people never do ask it. Others don't ask with perfect sincerity. They are not determined to do whatever He should ask them. We need never be afraid. *If we really want to please God we shall do so.* St. Thomas Aquinas, on being asked the shortest way to love God, said: "To

want to love Him." If we want to overcome pride, obstinacy, sloth, we shall do
so. If in the past I have been conceited
and selfish and if I want to overcome these
faults in the future, I can do so.

✠   **DON'T BLAME GOD**   ✠

WE cannot all be intimate with the aristocracy. Many of us seem to feel
that those laws which hold good in
social life apply also to the spiritual life.
That it is only a certain select few who
are really called upon to love God, to become intimate with our Lord. That for
the ordinary mortal such an idea is pure
presumption. We look up to loving God
as we would look up to Mont Blanc. The
eternal snows bathed in sunshine, radiant,
stupendous, magnificent, but inaccessible
and unapproachable. And God is every
hour trying to draw you nearer to Him,
and you are trying to draw back. "Lord,
what wouldst Thou have me do?" First,
to be satisfied with your lot in life. Not
to want to be richer, cleverer, prettier.
Who is responsible for every detail of
your life? God. If you are discontented,
it is, in plain English, rebellion against
God's Will. Find me the person who is
absolutely satisfied and you will find a

saint. Let us make it a rule always to try
and be satisfied. What an effect it would
have on our lives. Wet or fine, ill or well,
rich or poor. Don't blame God. And
about my spiritual state? I ought to be
eager to get on; but even that I should
leave in His hands. Be satisfied even
with your spiritual state. If God does not
want you to go forward more quickly than
you are doing, do not wish to do so. He
does not wish us to become saints in a
day. He wishes a virtue to grow. Acting
up to grace means doing the easy things
that come our way, doing them well, and
doing them humbly because they are His
Will. Thus do we become saints.

✠   **SLOW AND DULL?**   ✠

IN the Gospel St. John tells how our
Lord cured the man who had lain for
no less than thirty-eight years by the pool,
waiting to be the first into the water after
the Angel had stirred it. When we think
of the years we have lived and the little
we have accomplished, may we not justly
compare ourselves with that poor man?
Year after year he fails to reach the water
first and, heaving a sigh, hopes for better
luck next time. Year after year we have
been slack in the service of God.

Are we not waiting for the moving of the water? When God sends His Angel to touch the pool of our soul, in which He should be, but is not always, mirrored, should we not listen to Him? Do we not often say: "It is hardly of any use my trying to reach the pool of God's grace. I may as well lie here. Others always get there first. I am too slow and dull to try. I have little belief in His love for and interest in me." We ought to say: "After all, it is not so difficult to love God. If He laid down His life for me, He must love me a little bit. If not a single thought passes through my mind that has not passed through God's mind, does it not show He cares for me?" Remorse is the lover's expostulation for not having trusted more.

✠   GOD THE TEACHER   ✠

THERE is only one person who can teach us to love God. Himself. If you do not think Him lovable, you cannot love Him. Religion is the service of God, is love of God. He is everything that is likeable, lovable, and easy to get on with. If you think Him haughty, far away and unapproachable, you invest Him with unlovable qualities and you certainly will not love Him.

The Devil says: "You are unfitted for His service, a coward. He offered you a mortification; you did not take it. You are weary in well-doing. You are not one of the *élite* called to Divine love." He wishes us to think of our Master as hard, difficult to please; that we must for ever be on our best behavior. How different from the Apostles, who were completely at home with Him. What is the talisman for the future? It is to have a true opinion of our Lord. Not to think Him difficult, pompous, hard, but generous, willing, ever eager to forgive and always finding more to pity than to blame in us. Ask our Lord to help us to know Him, for to know Him is to love Him.

☩   CHRIST'S HUMANITY   ☩

WE have difficulty in not looking at our Lord as a high and mighty Personage. We should try hard to realize that our Lord in His Humanity felt just as we feel. Tired, weary, hungry. When left alone, inclined to take a dismal view of life, tempted to despondency, our Lord likes us to show Him sympathy. He in His life on earth was just as appreciative of every particle of sympathy offered Him as we should be. Never the smallest kindness done to Him was unnoticed. He hungered for love and sympathy. In the house of Simon how He appreciated St. Mary Magdalene's ministrations. He said to Simon, who was pretending not to notice Mary Magdalene, "When I entered your house you gave Me no water for My feet. This woman with her tears has washed them, and with her hair has wiped them. You gave Me no kiss; this woman has never ceased to kiss My feet."

✠   IN DISAPPOINTMENT   ✠

WE do not realize how much our Lord bore for us. The one thing He desired when He came into the world was to do good to souls. If we have one great object in life, and that object is thwarted, what a crushing sorrow it is. And yet our Lord was thwarted at every turn. His preaching was misunderstood; His miracles and cures He got no thanks for. The one thing He looked for, to gain love, failed Him. Take our Lord's day; it was one long string of disappointments. And how we grumble over our trifling, futile, little disappointments. How ungenerous, how mean we are.

When you think of your disappointments, compare them with our Lord's. The

way to be happy is to look at things from
His point of view. His efforts invariably
met with failure. When He had explained
fully about His Body and Blood (John
vi.), we are told that "many of them
ceased to walk with Him." What a sorrow for Him! Then it was that, feeling
crushed and worn out, He said to St.
Peter: "Wilt thou also leave Me?" And
St. Peter answered: "To whom, Lord, shall
we go, for Thou hast the words of eternal
life?" What a disappointment even the
Apostles were. At the end even of the
third year of His ministry how imperfect
they were, how little credit they did Him.
They had arrived at no greater under-
standing of Him than to think still that
He was to be the Founder of an earthly
kingdom, and at no greater virtue than to
be wrangling as to who were to have the
best places.

✠   **ENOUGH FOR ME**   ✠

IF our Lord were to say to us: "I will,
if you choose it, give you a life of
perfect happiness; everyone shall try to
please you, everything you touch succeed,"
I trust there is no one here who would not
say: "No, Lord; what was good enough
for You is good enough for me." These

thoughts should throw a flood of light on our lives. If we wish to imitate our Lord and Master, instead of crying our eyes out in moments of gloom and despondency, we should say: "What Thou dost is for the best, I will not wish it otherwise. When I am cowardly and inclined to cry out under suffering; if I ask for the pain to be removed — do not take me at my word, Lord, but give me greater strength and so draw me nearer to Thee."

☩   BUCKLER OF HOPE   ☩

"EVERY word of God is fire-tried, and He is a Buckler of Hope to those who hope in Him." This means that every word of God is absolutely true, and that He is a shield or protector to those who hope in Him. What is the hope most people have in Him? Withered, shrunk, ineffective. (I am not, of course, speaking of the theological virtue on which our salvation depends, but of hope in God's help in the every-day episodes of our life.) Religion should be a part of one's life. It consists in always thinking of God. The whole day long. Our Lord wants to be Master of your heart, and Master all the day long. Our Lord lives in your heart. He does not want you to tell Him in so many words that you love Him; He knows you cannot be praying all day. But He wants you always to be thinking of Him, to feel that He is with you.

People are not intimate with Him be· cause they *think* they can't be. So they don't try. Our Lord says: "My yoke is sweet and my burden is light." And again: "Come to Me all ye who labor and are burdened and I will refresh you." One condition He always asks: Trust. No matter how weak you are, how frail, He will help if you will only go to Him. If anyone would really believe that God would make him a saint he would become one. We should have bigger hearts, more confidence. We don't trust Him one-tenth part as much as we should. Where do any good thoughts or aspirations we ever have come from? From Him; they are His gift. He says: "If you will only let Me, I will make a saint of you." It is by your want of confidence, hope and trust, that you tie His hands.

✠   NEED OF SYMPATHY   ✠

THERE is hardly a greater power than sympathy. The craving for sympathy is an ornament to our nature: God does not mean us to stand alone. Our Lord

Himself craved for sympathy, especially in His Agony, but also throughout His life on earth: yet how bitterly did He suffer from the want of it! So may it often be with us. When we are suffering under any special unsatisfied craving of this kind, let us attach it to some particular want of sympathy endured by our Lord in the bitterness of His Sacred Passion.

✠   SOURCE OF SYMPATHY   ✠

TO have experienced lack of sympathy and to have learned to stand alone without it, should be of great value to us in our spiritual life:

If we do not get it on earth, we are forced to look from earth to heaven, for *there* we know is One Who cannot change, and Who knows perfectly all our sufferings and all our difficulties.

Indeed, there are certain natures with strong affections, of whom God seems to be jealous, desiring all that wealth of love for Himself. From them He withdraws all earthly sympathy, so that they are compelled to turn to Him, Who alone can satisfy them.

By wanting sympathy and not getting it, we learn by experience how to sympathize with others. No one is so well able to give sympathy as one who has known the want of it; one who wishes to save others from having to drink the cup which he himself has deeply drunk.

✠ MONOTONY: INJUSTICE ✠

WE must fight against our natural dislike of monotony by not casting our thoughts forward and thereby making the temptation stronger, foreseeing that to-morrow will be the same as to-day, and the next day the same as to-morrow, and so on.

Rather let us throw ourselves heartily into the work in hand, reminding ourselves that we know very little about the future, or even if we shall have a future, and making each day stand by itself as it were the last one. God intends us to find life monotonous for otherwise we should become too fond of it. It is one of His ways of bringing home to us our need of Him, and we should look on it and welcome it as a part of our education. The best cure for monotony in our own lives is to try to make the lives of others more bright and cheerful.

Can any injustice I shall ever have to suffer come up to those which our blessed Lord bore for my sake, and which He felt most acutely? For love of Him let us keep our lips closed when we smart under the sense of injustice. Two thoughts that will help us:

1. If we ourselves have ever been unjust to others, it behooves us not to be too sensitive when others seem to be unjust to us.

2. If we were all of us to receive perfect justice, "which of us would escape a whipping?" And should we then be so eager to put forward our claims?

✠   LITTLE SINS   ✠

CONSIDER the sinfulness of little sins, remembering that whether a sin be mortal or venial, the Person against Whom it is committed is the same.

They deprive us of the special providence and favor of God. By this special providence I mean that special care God takes of the soul in the midst of temptations; God keeping away difficulties; not allowing the Devil that power he would otherwise have; the felt companionship of God Himself.

In friendship a little matter may come between friends; so with God; if His friends do wilfully even some little thing against Him, He cannot help feeling it.

By little sins our spiritual senses become dulled. We do not see God in His creatures; in prayer we do not hear Him. If our hearing were good, God would only have to whisper and we should hear Him at once.

By little sins we lose, or never acquire, that briskness and energy in doing God's work which were characteristics of the saints, even in sickness and old age. And where is our longing to make ourselves better? Habitual venial sin is the enemy of all these things.

☩   GOD'S WILL   ☩

THE first condition for carrying out God's Will in our regard — the sanctification of our soul — is to believe we can do it.

Three thoughts to help us:

1. God is much more interested in our sanctification than we are ourselves. It is not man who goes to God first, but God who comes to man, and as a beggar in this matter. It is not we who woo our blessed Lord, but He is the Lover who woos us. He takes it as a wonderful condescension on our part if we love Him, *He cannot help loving us:* "Can a mother forget her child, so as not to have pity on

the son of her womb? And if she should forget, yet will not I forget thee. Behold, I have graven thee in My hands." (Isaias xlix. 15, 16.)

2. We sometimes think past sins, near or far, must make it hopeless for us ever to attain to perfection. It is quite the contrary — we are forgiven in such a way that they no longer raise any obstacles between us and God. It is quite false to think that God bears us a grudge on account of the past.

3. God has a personal and special love for me, against which no argument can stand. God realizes my weakness more than I do myself, pities me, and gives me any amount of time to correct my faults. Go back to the history of your life, make a chart of God's mercies, and you will see at what pains He has been about you.

⊦   **GOD IS SHY**   ⊦

A SAINT'S sorrow is never in the way. There is about it a softness, a gentleness, a beauty; it is a cross only to himself. We must be careful, in sorrow, not to *demand* sympathy from others, and if possible not to crave for it. What is it worth if it comes when we have demanded it? There is no balm in it when

it is paid to us as a tax.   Surely the
preciousness lies in its being spontaneous.
This is not so much a question of what is
right or wrong, as of what is fittest and
best, of what God loves most, of what
makes sorrow most heavenly.   The more
consolation from creatures, the less from
God.   That is the invariable rule.   God
is shy; He comes to the lonely heart which
other loves do not fill.   This is why
bereaved hearts, outraged hearts, hearts
misunderstood, hearts which have broken
with kith and kin and native place, are the
hearts of His predilection.   Human sympathy is a dear bargain.   God waits outside till our company has gone.

✠   DIVINE DIRECTION   ✠

LOSE no opportunity in bringing home
to yourself our Lord's particular individual love of you, shown in even the
smallest details of your life.

It is God's peculiar prerogative, because
He alone is infinitely wise and all-power-
ful, to be able so to direct and rule each
single life as if that person alone was the
centre of the universe.

When I rise in the morning I can say
with truth: "This day, in all its circumstances, with all its consequences, has been

appointed and fashioned to help me to love and serve God better." Then you have only to fall in with your change of duties, or with the state of your health, or with the conduct of others towards you (which all has been foreseen and allowed for by God), secure in the knowledge that you are travelling along the path whereby God Himself wishes you to approach Him.

✠   MAN'S CRAVING   ✠

MAN'S craving always has been to see God, to think he is near Him, as far as possible to get in touch with Him; and therefore the aim of religion is to know God, to get upon intimate terms with Him, to see Him in all the ordinary actions of our lives, to live for Him, and to ask His help.

This recognition of God is the chief duty of man.

It constitutes our supreme happiness — this reaching forth beyond ourselves. This impulse to put forth our hand into the darkness to grasp the hand of our Divine Savior, is common to all the human race, implanted in us by God Himself.

God is always calling to us, always beckoning to us, and thus always giving us a proof of His interest in us.

He is intended to be, He must always be, our Supreme Love. Of course He wishes us to find joy in this world, in the pure love of our fellow-creatures as well, if they do not shut out Him, and do not lead us into bondage to them. But even so, their power is only for a time; we wake as from a dream, and the old ache comes back, the old feeling of emptiness and dissatisfaction gnaws at our heart, and once more the cry breaks forth from our inmost being (very often a cry which we don't understand), "It is not enough, I need more; only show me God, show me my Lord and my God."

☩   GOD'S ANSWER   ☩

IN answer to this demand God, as we all know, came upon earth, and came in human form, spoke with a human voice, had a human appearance, because He was really man. He moved up and down in Palestine, and wherever He went He was loved, except by those who for political and other reasons were His enemies. He was so humble, so simple, so accessible to everyone, that even His enemies said: "The whole world has gone out after Him." Yet they who had seen Him and heard Him could not and would

not believe that the Lord of heaven and
earth could have come down into our
world, and have dwelt here, and have
hung upon the Cross until He was dead,
simply through love of them.   But it was
true. They disbelieved His love because it
was so great.

✠   **STILL ON EARTH**   ✠

THAT same God is in the world still.
He is in the world to-day although we
have not the privilege which they had, who
lived along with Him, of seeing Him with
our bodily eyes and listening to His human voice.

Our Lord is in the tabernacle of every
Catholic church; we cannot see His fea-
tures, nor His shape, but beneath the veil
of bread His Sacred Body is there as truly
as it was in Nazareth.   He is with us
wholly and entirely in His perfect Man-
hood, in His eternal Divinity.   He does
not indeed usually work miracles of heal-
ing men's bodies as He did then, but now
He cures souls, and when He comes, as
He does at Holy Communion, He is God
still.   He always was God, He is God,
and if you go to Him as you ought — if
you go to Him with faith, with love, and
with a contrite heart, He is ready, when

He enters into your bosom, to take you to His own. That Body, against which the multitudes pressed by the banks of the Jordan, has now become your food: It nourishes you unto Life Everlasting.

✠   THE HEALING CHRIST   ✠

AS when He was on earth, those who went to Him with bodily diseases were cured by Him, we bring to Him now the diseases of the soul.

Come to Him in your darkness, in your sorrow, in your weakness, with your habits of self-indulgence, it may be, which have made your life a burden to you, and He will break the bonds.

He is God. He can do everything. Lay down before Him the burden of all your cares. Don't think He doesn't understand all about yourself. He alone does thoroughly understand you, because He made you, soul and body. He will either charm your sorrows away, or give you strength of mind and body to bear them. You will never find Him disappointing. He has all knowledge and all power, and He loves you more than you can believe.

You find life lonely. You find life with no relish in it. Go to Him, and He will make your life full of meaning, full of joy.

And now you will ask: "How am I to find in Him a friend? I want a friend badly, and one who won't change with the weather. A friend who will do me good. Someone to protect me in my hidden trials, who will always be patient with me, who will never tire of me when I am so tired of myself."

✠ SHORTEST CUT ✠

GO to Him; but go to Him not only as to one who has a human heart, but who is also Very God of Very God.

Go to Him as to one who loves you, and if you only understand that a little better, it will explain everything and make everything easy.

Don't think that He requires you to stand on ceremony with Him. You cannot be too simple, too childlike, too direct.

Why will you not believe His own speech? Why should He say He loves you if He does not do so in fact?

The shortest way to the mind and heart of God is to take Him at His word. A saint is a person who believes God's promises literally, and trusts them entirely and always.

What is the explanation of this great mystery?

God Who framed the heavens, caresses
with baby hands the sweet face of His
Mother — a woman — His own creature!
He has made Himself a home upon earth!

Why was His infinite Power attracted
by our weakness? Why was His Pity
greater than our wilfulness? Why has
His Purity cleansed our sins? How was it
that the Creator and the creature, Perfection and imperfection, Light and darkness,
were thus brought together?

Not by constraint, because no one can
constrain Almighty God. Not in His
Wisdom, nor in His Greatness, nor in His
Justice, will you find written the secret—
why God created us, and dwelt and dwells
amongst us.

One little word holds it all: the highest,
dearest, best of all words; another word
for God Himself — *Love! God is Love.*

Approach Him by love; abide with Him
in love. He wants you to live with Him
now; to make a Friend of Him now.

✠ LOOKING FOR TROUBLE ✠

THERE is a danger sometimes of a sort
of Jansenism creeping into our spiritu-
ality, an idea that we must never be happy
or satisfied unless we are unhappy. It is
true there is a good deal of suffering in the

world, but it is a pity to be looking in every hole and corner to find it. It is a mistake to think that every little accident and contretemps — even too much salt in the soup — is a design of Providence, specially brought about for the benefit of our souls. It is true that in the case of a few mystical saints God has sent very special trials, but as a rule, with those who are striving to serve Him faithfully, God's direction is wonderfully mild. Don't take it into your head that every little accident is devised for your special torture. It is a false, incorrect view to imagine that you cannot be pleasing to God unless you are always suffering. As a rule, the outward life of a saint is very much like everybody else's. There are the contradictions that come inevitably. A good life is always a sort of reproach to those who don't lead it, and that brings opposition. If we try to push forward God's cause, of course the Devil will try to oppose us.

✠   DON'T BE MORBID   ✠

DON'T think there is any virtue in suffering as suffering. Don't be morbid! It was all in the day's work in the case of the saints. Remember suffering was not intended from the beginning: there are

plenty of things God *permits* but does not
wish; certainly we should never be indifferent to the sufferings of others, but try
to diminish them as much as possible.

✠ A FALSE IDEA ✠

ST. PAUL says, "Rejoice in the Lord
always, and again I say, rejoice."
(Phil. iv. 4.) If we want to serve God, joy
should be not only an element, it should be
the staple of our life. Our difficulties are
so great, our enemies so many, that unless
we are supported by joy, we shan't do
what God wants us to do. It is a point
of great consequence. There is a sort of
impression that in the service of God
there ought to be a certain sobriety, an
earnestness — yes, *sadness,* which makes
the distinction between the service of the
world, and the service of God; and that
those who serve God must expect more
tribulation and uneasiness of mind. Entirely false. St. Paul, speaking under the
dictation of the Holy Spirit, says, "Rejoice, again I say, rejoice." If we think
the ideal of a religious person is to be sad,
it is quite wrong, it is the direct opposite
to the truth. We are never so much fitted
to cope with the difficulties of the spiritual
life as when we are in joy.

Read carefully the Acts of the Apostles:
no one can read them without being struck
by the spirit of buoyancy and exaltation
that fills and pervades them; one might
almost call it high spirits. The Apostles
carried their lives in their hands; they were
scourged, and came forth from their severe
flogging full of joy, rejoicing they were
found worthy to suffer for their Lord. We
certainly then can't be doing wrong in
making our lives lives of joy.

✠   A COMMON ERROR   ✠

IT is a common error — that God sends
us trials for their own sake. Looking on pain and trouble as good things is
not a sound view. It does us harm by
making us think God takes pleasure in
seeing us suffer. The greatest possible
happiness to be got out of life is in the
service of God. God doesn't like to see
us cry, even though it is good for us. It
pains God for me to suffer pain — that is
a lovable and *true* view of God. To
think of the Passion as God heaping tor-
ments on His Son is Jansenist.

Taking our lives as they are, and being
happy in them, is a true way to perfection.
Very few crosses are *directly* sent by God.
God permits them, but they come from

someone, or something else, or from ourselves — being disappointed in something
we had aimed at. We should cut down
our estimate of what God really sends us
very considerably.

✠   **WHAT GOD WANTS**   ✠

WHAT does He want of me? He wants
you to take your life as it is, bearing
your trials and disappointments as quietly
as you can. Empty lamentings over things
not being as they ought to be, must be
eschewed. The way to make things better
is not to be doleful, but happy and cheerful. "Your joy no man shall take from
you . . . (John xvi. 22) Our life is as it
is: in that I am to find the material for
serving God. Supposing even my trials
are my own fault *really* — the results of
my own actions staring me in the face. If
I can't put it to rights, let me be sorry for
what is wrong and go on cheerfully. Start
afresh. The service of God is from hour
to hour and from day to day. If things
are going contrary, it is a pity to be thinking we have great crosses and trials, and
bemoaning ourselves: the way to do work
for God is to be full of happiness . . . No
heart was ever so tender as the Heart of
our Lord: He couldn't see a person weep

without wanting to stop their tears.—Then how am I to account for my life being so full of misery?—*Is* it all as I think? If the fault is in myself, it is hard to put it all on God.—You don't think your temper, for instance, comes down straight from God?—God respects our free will. Should we like to be milksops in God's service?

✠   STAPLE OF SERVICE   ✠

WE need not be dissatisfied if we have no special trial; bearing with our wretched bodies and souls is the staple of our service to God. *"Traffic till I come."* (Luke xix. 13.) Bear the cross and all your difficulties well — don't make much of them. We ought to be ashamed to run like children with a hurt finger for sympathy and consolation in every little trouble. God loves His own as the apple of His eye. Bear all, then, in love and patience for His sake.

We must get out of our heads the idea that we can only be religious by being miserable. If you will think of God as difficult and unapproachable, — if you are afraid of Him, and think He is high and haughty, and far away from you, you won't love Him. One of the ruses of the Devil, whenever we fall short of the highest standard, is to tell us: "You are not one of those chosen souls who are called to love God." You must think of Him as one who knows our poor, craven natures. He knows it all seems flat and monotonous, and that you feel weary of well-doing. It will all pass: our Lord hasn't abandoned you. Hold on—it will all come right again.

✠   LITTLE CROSSES   ✠

SUFFERING which comes to us from God is best; and that comes to us through our circumstances, our surroundings, ourselves, and those we live with: these come from God, being permitted by Him. They are the warp and woof of our spiritual life. If you want to become solidly virtuous, your life from moment to moment gives you occasions of bearing lovingly for God's sake any amount of suffering. People forget to sanctify the daily little crosses or life; they must be big and marked with a red cross, that we may recognize they come from God. But we can't get away from these little crosses and mortifications, they are woven into our life — a clear sign they come from God.

Do we receive crosses as a great deal less than we deserve? Do we take them in a spirit of resignation, and a sense of their justice? Shouldn't we eliminate a good many altogether, if we did this? Our limitations, of nature, position, intellectual gifts, are very real mortifications and crosses; but if we have some realization of what we have deserved for our sins, we shan't be lost in admiration of our patience, but we shall accept them quite naturally.

✠   A HARDER IDEAL   ✠

THERE is nothing so good for the education of character as having something to bear. It brings out all that is best in us. If I have all I can desire, excellent food and lodging, and no cares and anxieties, what is there to try my temper? What is there to admire in me, if I am amiable and cheerful under these circumstances? We admire those who, in spite of difficulties, bear their burdens cheerfully and unselfishly, thinking of others' sorrows rather than their own. How, then, shall we carry out what we believe of the value of suffering into our daily life, and let it, as it ought, bring out what is great and noble in our characters?

We must have a *harder* ideal, and profit by the difficulties of life. Wouldn't it be well to *act* upon what we acknowledge in theory to be excellent? Our good God

desires us to have happiness in His service.
Often you will see that the heavier the
cross, the lighter is the step, and the more
cheerful the countenance with which it is
borne.   Why let yourself be so easily dis-
turbed?   What are you worrying about?
You are not living with saints and angels,
you are not one yourself.   It is a blessing
to be rid of the crosses coming by your
own fault, but those that God sends, accept them gladly.   God allows natural
laws to create difficulties, and then helps
us to overcome them.   Confide in God.

✠   CHRIST'S EXAMPLE   ✠

TO some will come at times a taste of
that horrible perplexity our Lord
had in the Garden of Olives.   At times it
will seem almost impossible to do what
we know God wants us to do.   There was
a moment when our Lord seemed to waver
and balance as to whether He would go on
with His Passion.   It must cost us something, if we mean to do something memorable for God.   That is the time of the
greatest anguish of mind, when we are
balancing the question.   Thereafter came
that complete calm which our Lord never
lost during His Passion, save in that
moment of His dereliction on the Cross.

The Devil does his best to mislead us. He says, if you were able to do it, you wouldn't have all this extraordinary difficulty. On the contrary, the disturbance comes from the world, the flesh, and the Devil, and they wouldn't make such a stir if the matter were not so important. Therefore, when we have to take resolutions which cost us much, let us look at the Garden of the Agony, and take comfort from our Lord. And observe, all was in the natural course of events, God allowing creatures to work out their designs. We need not think He interposed to provide special ignominy for our Lord.

☩   STRENGTH TO ENDURE   ☩

WHEN the conflict has ceased, and Our Lord had fully accepted the sacrifice, He was perfectly self-possessed. Let us too be calm, and united with God, and that will give us strength and endure that suffering we had dreaded and shrunk from. To all outward appearances our Lord's life was a failure; so will it often be with us. Yet it is just then we are most like Him, and in our very failure will lie our success in the sight of God.

Our Lord's Agony was an anticipation of suffering: specially helpful in these

days, so full of subjective troubles. "My
soul is sorrowful even unto death." (Matt.
xxvi. 38.)   A sadness of itself such as to
produce death. His soul, generally in such
peace and calm, was taken possession of
by suffering that was enough to take His
life. What was the cause? The knowledge, the anticipation of His Passion. "He
began to fear and to be heavy" (Mark
xiv. 33) — a sickness of heart — agony
— fear. Jesus was mortally sad. This
fact ought to be of the greatest comfort
and consolation to us. To find a parallel
to our sufferings in the Blessed Son of
God is a lifelong asset of consolation that
can't be prized too highly.

☩   **PROOF OF LOVE**   ☩

IF the perfect soul of our Lord could,
without grossest injustice, be so
dimmed by sadness that there and then
the soul might have parted from the body,
what right have you or I to think our lot
hard? Whatever our trial is, the thought
ought to follow us all day, whether our
trouble be physical or mental. When I
am sad, I am only undergoing the same
experience as my Lord and Master.
    Much less is it wrong that I should
undergo this sadness. It is the very best

proof of love I can give Him, and if it
knits me nearer to Him, I ought to look
upon it as a gift from God.

☩   SERVING WELL   ☩

I AM never serving God so well as
when I am bearing the Cross, standing under its shadow. Some of us think
that if we feel sad when we have something to do for God which is hard and
unpleasant, we are doing wrong. If my
sorrow comes from anticipated trouble,
my Lord's sorrow was from the same
cause. . . The Devil likes us not to humble
ourselves, because when the saints did it
they were exalted as if they were walking
on air . . . When our Lord came to grips
with His pain, He did pray, "If it be possible, let this chalice pass from me." (Matt.
xxvi. 39.) When we have no courage, the
Devil says, "Go back." *No; go on.* It is
nonsense to say the mortifications of the
saints cost them nothing. To feel dreadfully afraid, and as if we cannot do what
we have made up our minds to do, proves
nothing. Remember our Lord's prayer.
Finding Himself in this dreadful depression, He set Himself to pray, and cast
Himself down on His face.

The repulsion was so great, it set up a

kind of wrestling—a struggle, that brought a pressing of the blood from the veins in such abundance that it soaked His garments, and dropped on the grass. Some people think that the saints drank down pain like a sweet draught. A mistake. Our Lord *shrank* from the pain presented to Him. The use of the will had to be so strong that His whole Body was bathed in blood.

He began "to be afraid." (Mark xiv. 33.) Fear seized upon Him by His own permission. He was pale, and shudders went through His Body. There is nothing so terrible as to see men afraid. They seem to lose the power of guiding themselves. It might have seemed impossible that our Lord should have felt fear. If, with great reverence, we could watch Him — how He stoops for love of us! Learn from this that fearing our trouble is no sign of unfaithfulness to God.

✠   **ABIDING COMFORT**   ✠

(M)EANWHILE He prays. His trial consisted in putting aside the consolation He might have had. What makes our darkness so dense is that God does not let us have the consolations we had expected to feel in time of trial.

An angel appeared, strengthening and comforting Him. We come away from the Tabernacle perhaps without an atom of consolation or sweetness, but He always strengthens and encourages us.

✠   MY IMPORTANCE   ✠

THERE is no such thing as "the world" to God. Each one of us is a world to Him. It is a mistake not to think half enough of ourselves. To think of ourselves in "general" is an imperfect way of thinking. We each cost the Eternal Son of God His Blood. We are so important to God, we carry out His Will. In spite of my sins and imperfections, God follows all my history with incessant care and interest. What does it matter if in this year I am a little better or a little worse? In God's eye a great deal. It is not only possible, but practicable, for us all to make a mark in Divine History. Acts of virtue, acts of love of Him will make me memorable for ever and ever.

The thought of this, and the effort to fulfil it will color my grey life, and make me ashamed if I dare to think it empty. My poor life is of the utmost value in God's eyes. We must try to realize our nearness to God, and His claims upon us.

One great privilege of the spiritual life is,
there is no time in it. The intensity of an
act needs no time, and one moment can
hold more than ten years.

There is more danger of our not hoping
enough than of our hoping too much.
Don't put your standard so low. If you
want to go high, the higher the things you
think God wants of you, the better.
Breathe the air of God's promises, and
raise your hearts high. God wants a
great deal of us. You have never hitherto believed that He really does. You say
to yourself, if God wanted me to be a saint,
He should have given me a very different
character. Whether you are a Carmelite
or living in the world, there is not the
smallest difference in the love God wants
of you. Please, remember that!

✠   THE BEST GIFT   ✠

HITHERTO I have not realized what
God wants of me. The highest gifts
of prayer, what are they compared to the
gift of His Body and Blood! When He
asks us to look up and see His face, we
will look down. When He wants us to
walk forward, we *will* shut our ears to His
invitation. Difficulties will vanish at once
if we can only bring ourselves to believe

that God loves us so. Unconquerable Hope
in spite of apparent difficulty. Don't let
your heart sink with the false feeling that
"somehow God doesn't care specially for
me." The saints combined humility with
the unshaken belief in God's great personal
and individual love for them.

✠ SELF-MASTERY ✠

WE ought not to lose heart when we find
there are plenty of occasions on which
we might very well practise mortification
— and don't.

It is much better to take two eggs and
say to yourself, "How unmortified I am!"
than to take only one and wonder how
soon it will be before you are canonized.
Honesty is another name for humility
sometimes, and if only you are honest,
you'll very likely get so thoroughly
ashamed of yourself that you'll get mor-
tified and do with no egg at all. If you
are dishonest with yourself, you'll never
get on: *not* to practise mortification, and
then to find false reasons for our neglect,
is bad.

Saint Paul said: "I chastise my body
and bring it into subjection." (1 Cor. ix.
27.) But we should not be discouraged
because we can't carry out much bodily

austerity, or think that on that account we can't hope to get very near to God.

Self-mastery has no *necessary* connection with bodily austerity. What is wanted is the subduing of the spirit: the body counts for nothing. But if the body is a difficulty and a hindrance to this end, we must bring it into subjection.

When God wants great bodily mortification He makes a soul know it, and gives the desire for it so strongly that the soul would suffer more by *not* doing it than it does in the austerity.

✠ REAL AUSTERITY ✠

OU ask, is it possible for *me* to be a true servant of God without performing wonderful austerities? Yes, great grace is often given without great bodily penance: the Little Flower of Jesus is an instance of this.

It is no small penance in these days merely to bear with yourself; and if you bear properly with yourself and with your neighbor, God will give you the highest graces.

Don't be idiotic! When you have found this or that disturbance produced by a fit of nerves, don't straightway fancy something is wrong with your soul. You are being carried away by false notions and making a great mistake if you think you can't *be* good because you don't *feel* good. To feel "rotten," and yet have patience with yourself, remaining quiet and keeping your recollection; to maintain evenness of temper; not to be influenced by changing moods; to be always serene; this is to practise real austerity and high virtue.

☩   WHEN DEPRESSED   ☩

☉HE feeling of depression, when all faith and hope seem lost, and we can't do anything, is a great trial. But to endure it patiently is great virtue.

Read Saint Teresa with intelligence: she says the most trying part of sickness is the inability to fix our thoughts on God. But she says we must not let that matter: the important thing is to submit to the will of God, to accept our sickness with patience, and suffer for God even if we cannot keep our thoughts fixed on Him.

Indigestion, ennui, bodily weakness, are often more difficult to bear properly than bodily austerity.

Accept your sickness from God, and in these black hours be very content to have Him and no other as a witness to your pains of body and of mind.

And don't talk to everybody about your health, and, above all, about your nerves. To hear some people talk, you would think they didn't believe God knows what nerves are.

If you can't do more than suffer in silence, be willing not to do more. If you know some one who acts in this way, you know some one who is pleasing to God.

✠   FORBEARANCE   ✠

OUR neighbor. Most of us have a good deal to put up with from our neighbors, yet we generally forget what they have to put up with from us.

Still, we have difficulties even with very good people. They are not omniscient, they often make mistakes, and they treat us according to their ideas. It is a part of the way in which God wishes to sanctify us.

Conceited as we are, we should be much worse if we were not corrected by others. There are many excellent parts in our characters, but some dreadful gaps. We are like trees that have not grown straight. If we would let our Lord have His way, and bear with what He does for us through our neighbor, we should grow more symmetrical.

Why are we not more considerate? Why do we form such harsh judgments? Here have we great scope for true austerity.

✠   MINISTERING   ✠

THE Angels are our models. It would be an excellent encomium on our lives if we could claim some title to the name of ministering spirit. "Ministering spirits" — minister — what is a minister? One in a lower position, a servant. Our Lord said He had come not to be ministered to but to minister; He Himself had come to labor. The more blessed thing is not to have authority, but to be under others. When we arrange plans, somehow or other we are always leader in the work to be done. To be under others, working for others, is so much more pleasing to God.

I am put in the world to be a servant. So many of my troubles are concerned with what I consider my due: not to be under, but above. When we are out of humor, why are we distressed? Isn't it often our wanting to be above others? We can't admit that to ourselves, we don't *want* it, we say, it *must* be so. We are meant to do work. Am I to be allowed to be head, or to work under others? When I am inclined to shrug my shoul-

ders and say, "there's no work for me to
do," what do I mean? Am I useful? What
good have I done to others? This world
is palpitating with misery and need of
every kind. Am I one of the great unem-
ployed in God's service? Are there no
broken hearts to bind up, no family difficulties to smooth over? I needn't draw
attention to myself — though that is the
very thing I want. As to the humdrum
work of every day, — not insisting on my
rights, bearing troubles quietly, etc.—how
much have I done? There is not much
difficulty in finding people to do conspic-
uous work. Those who are humble bear
God's universe. I am intended to minister. God must choose my work, and He
speaks by circumstances. We are surrounded by exactly the persons most fitted
to enable us to work out our salvation, the
path lies straight before us. Don't try to
be put forward, but do your work — nothing out of the common — well and
cheerfully, and with thankfulness to God.

✠   **YOUR LINE?**   ✠

I MUST work in any capacity; if in
obscurity, so much the better. Whatever our position, we are all ministering
spirits. The angels always work, day and

night: they watch all the incidents of our life, hear all we say, love us with a marvellous love, take the keenest interest in us, unselfishly, for their reward is only that we serve God better. Nor are they less zealous because of our ingratiude. Let us endeavor to imitate them by ministering. To anyone who folds his arms and says "It is not in my line," I ask, "What is in your line?"

If the *Son of God* came to minister, I should have thought *we* might find it a privilege to be allowed to minister in any form whatever.

✠ **NORMAL CONDITION** ✠

THE only class who can hear themselves praised without satisfaction, or blamed without displeasure, are the saints. A saint with a habit of humility doesn't look upon a slight with distress.

But we, who are not saints, or not yet saints, when we receive a snub are disappointed; we feel sore; that is inevitable, and we ought to accept it as our own normal condition.

You make a resolution: "I will never be proud any more." And then you are miserable at a thought of vanity. Why are you so stupid? Of course, your reso-

lution flies. I wish there were a recipe for
thinking oneself into humility. God
never finds fault with what we can't help.
I can't help having the feelings, but don't
let me give way to depression in consequence. The feelings won't harm me.
Then, if I feel stirrings of jealousy, is it
a conclusion that I am to remain in that
condition? Bear the jealous feeling quietly,
and by degrees that will make you humble.
If you pretend you have no feelings, you
are rebelling against facts, and that is only
a continuance of pride. You are on the
high road to humility when you confess
to yourself that you are horribly jealous,
and take it quietly. Be patient.

⊹   **HUMAN RESPECT**   ⊹

YOU show you are proud, because you
are in a hurry to be humble. Do
you know if you *were* humble, you would
be a saint? When you have done something particularly proud, leave it alone.
Or something very gauche; leave it alone.
The less you think on what you have said
the better. The recipe is exceedingly
simple. You'll find the impression gradually depending in your mind, What a conceited wretch I am! If you are sorry you
have cut an unfavorable figure, leave it

alone. If you brood on it you will soon feel, "I am not sorry because I have offended God, but because I have lost my self-respect, or forfeited the good opinion of some one"; and that is neither contrition nor humility.

✠   PARLOR SAINTS   , ✠

WHAT are you doing for God? People examine their consciences at night to see if they have offended God. But have you loved God? served God? conquered yourself? helped your neighbor? "Oh no, but I have avoided distractions — and to do so I say as few prayers as possible." You have joined that Association for helping your neighbor? "Oh no, I find it distracts me, and gives occasion to me to go into a passion." It is much better to do good, and be guilty of faults, than not to do good and commit fewer faults.

Saint Mechtilde thanked God for preserving her from the temptations to which the poor priests who preached were subject. The saint had belonged to a great family in the world, and our Lord said to her: "My daughter, you must have noticed, when your father's hounds came in from the chase, how they were all covered with mud and froth, etc., and your mother

would never have suffered them in the
drawing-room. Yet poodles were there.
Which of them were the better dogs?
Which did the master of the house value
most?" . . . Those who give themselves up
to the service of God might well have con-
tracted little stains, even mud, blood, etc.,
but they are of much greater worth than
those who, sleek and clean, have been sit-
ting at home doing nothing.

✠ NOTHING TO DO? ✠

NOW shall we avoid an accumulation
of *debt* for venial sin? A person who
tries to work for God will have a much
smaller debt than one who leads a nega-
tive, colorless life. What about sins of
omission? What are you going to answer
when you realize for the first time the good
you might have done in the world, and
have not done? Every one has his own
place in the world, and acts and reacts on
others: we are all members of one family.
A sin of omission is not fulfilling that mis-
sion which God has given us to do.

Remember the man who had only one
talent and hid it in the ground. What a
hard judgment he had! God has given us
all a talent. You say you have nothing
to do in the world? It is very odd that

God should have put you here with nothing to do. You needn't start another religious Order. There is always work to be done. You may be perfectly certain you are not in the world for nothing. If it's only to make your home happy, and bear the trials God sends you, — that's not only avoiding evil, it's doing good. Am I growing into that stature God intended for me? That is a very home question for us all to ask ourselves. Why have I not exerted a better influence? Am I falling short of God's purpose in creating me and putting me here?

✠ ESSENCE OF PRAYER ✠

IT is not the solitude of the Himalayas that makes prayer. The essence of prayer is the company of our Lord. The more we understand that He is everywhere present, that He is within us, that we are always in the presence of God, the more easily we pray. There is no peace of soul so great as that given by the thought of the presence of God. Whether you think of it or not, He is always there. If you want to learn, ask our Lord to teach you to pray. "But who am I that I should ask so great a thing?" You are only one of those for whom our Lord laid down His life, and of whom He is always thinking, day and night — to whom He gives Himself every morning in the Holy Eucharist. So I do not see where the impertinence of the request comes in. Ask Him: He will like nothing better.

✠ **WASTED TIME** ✠

HOW much time is lost in useless regrets; I have made a fool of myself —even done something wrong—wasting time instead of going back straight to God with an act of contrition. Never go back on the past. Don't stop, thinking over something foolish you have done or said and regretting it. We are very poor creatures, and there is nothing so wise as to live in the present.

Another fruitful waste of time is day dreaming: holding imaginary conversations, or fancying ourselves in positions where we play a very satisfactory part. It softens the mind.

Another is fussing. Fussing never saved time. A very celebrated surgeon, on the point of performing a critical operation, is said to have addressed the students about him with: "Now, gentlemen, don't let us hurry, because we have no time to lose." There are some people who are never quite self-possessed — always in a flurry. You know the saying, "If you want a letter answered, write to a busy man." These people hurry to Mass, hurry to meditation, hurry to breakfast, hurry all day long. A saint couldn't remain a saint under those conditions. Hurry is an enemy to the interior life.

☩   **SANCTITY EASY**   ☩

SANCTITY is easier than we suspect People *will say,* "It is not for the likes of me." If people unfortunately won't be-tie His hands. Surely our Lord wants your friendship. Don't tie His hands. "Of course, our Lord can't ask that of *me."* Many would be quite willing if only they could bring themselves to believe our Lord is asking it of them.

What makes a saint is a very tiny spark of the love of God. It suddenly strikes me that God really loves me, and that, if I don't do that little thing, it hurts Him.

If you try to serve Him out of love, He puts up with blunders, sulkiness, frail-ties, etc. There are plenty in the world who'll work out of love; many will do for another what they won't do for themselves.

How long it took the saints to become
saints: what disappointments they had!
Yet every one was persuaded that our
Lord loved them.   Never be afraid of desiring the highest graces.   Even the higher
kinds of prayer — there is no room for
vanity — no one need ever know anything at all about it.

✠   WHERE GOD IS   ✠

SOME people look for God anywhere
but at home, in their everyday clothes
and humdrum life. Every work we have to
do is God's.   We quite forget, though
God is in heaven, He is in my heart and
soul, and as much in my kitchen as in my
drawing-room.   Don't let us dream our
lives away, or wait for some great occasion of sacrifice which may never come.
"Oh, if only I had the facilities another
person has, what a wonderful person I
should be!"   A fallacy.   Your sanctity
consists in dealing with your present circumstances.   Do those things which are
close under your eyes and God will give
you more to do.

The saints became saints by using the
opportunities which others disdain. "God
couldn't have meant me to do such a work
in my circumstances."   We can leave that

to God quite safely, and if I allow Him to direct me, all will come right. To be willingly where we ought to be, attracts to us the invitation of our Lord.

Let us pray to grow in simplicity and the *desire* to see Him which is the prelude to His coming. If we long, He will satisfy our longing. Wherever we are, God will come to us, if He finds us trying to perfect. Desire Him to come as He has never come before. Offer Him the homage of rejoicing and offer Him your heart, desiring to be rid of failings and shortcomings.

✠   DISTRACTIONS   ✠

WHAT *is* a distraction? Those who un- understand them, don't bother about them. (I am speaking, of course, to those who are really striving to serve God.) A distraction is a wilful turning of the mind away from God. If we are talking with some one, and we deliberately turn away and look out of the window, it would be a serious breach of manners, of which no well-bred person would be guilty. If we don't do this with our friends, why should we do it with God? The fact is, we *don't.*

I put down to these imaginary distrac- tions the difficulty good people find in prayer. "How are you getting on?" "Not

at all, Father, my prayer is nothing but
distractions. How can I pretend I love
God? If I read a book, or talk to a friend,
my attention does not wander." Convers-
ing with God is more difficult because you
have not your senses to help you, nor an
answering voice. But your distraction is
absolutely inculpable, and does not interfere with the fruit of your prayer, unless
deliberately, of your own accord, and
when you can quite well do differently,
you turn away your thoughts from God
to something else. It is very unlikely any
good person would do it. How much we
are at the mercy of incoming thoughts!
Sometimes we seem the centre of a whirl-
wind of thought we cannot govern.

✠   **A SNARE**   ✠

MOST distractions are not distractions
at all. I am talking of what is
culpable in God's sight. If you would
only make up your mind that God doesn't
care anything about them! Few things
are so bad as to find so many excellent
people put off by this snare of the Devil.
It is useful to learn how little control we
have over our own thoughts. If you have
a great sorrow, or have received some injury, or some great temporal misfortune,

I defy you to keep it out of your thoughts.
Distractions are nothing to be afraid of.
As you are outside the chapel, so you will
be inside. You can't believe our Lord is
angry with you, because you haven't a
mind you can turn off and on at will.

✠   **A HUMAN WAY**   ✠

DON'T confess distractions unless you
are sure they are wilful. Write
off distractions permanently. At the same
time remember there is nothing about
which we should give ourselves so little
quarter as *wilful* distractions. Any turning away of your heart from God displeas-
es Him. Distractions don't interfere with
our union with God. Do you think when
He gives Himself to you in Holy Communion that our Lord inquires what we
are thinking about before He will do us
any good and that you make a barren,
profitless Communion in a time of great
sorrow, or if your mind is full of some
recent injury? "I have been thinking of
it all the time — what an awful sacrilege!"
Not at all — you are acting in a human
way, and our Lord doesn't care a bit about
it. If your intention of serving Him is the
same, you are praying all the time. Your
love is shown by what you do

Gradually one's whole nature gets leavened. Acting up to grace means doing what is easy at first — a little, day by day. But to say "I'll mortify myself in all possible circumstances—always sit up straight — tumble the mustard into the soup," we can't go on with it. Then the Devil says, "I told you so, you can't be a saint." Do a little, and do it humbly, and God will help you to go from little to greater things. . .

✠   "BE YE PERFECT"   ✠

OU think you crave very much for God's special presence; I daresay you do to a certain extent, but God is so generous, and wants us to love Him far more than we wish to love Him, and so it would be unreasonable if He refused us. But there is a want of preparation, a want of showing God our earnestness in the matter. A child wouldn't understand what a jewel was; all "pebbles" to him. That we should appreciate the difference requires some knowledge.

It is the same in the spiritual life. "I have been trying for these graces for years." Are you sure you value them as much as you think? Have I that appreciation of God's gifts, that longing for graces which shall make the practice of virtue easier, which I think I have? "The presence of God," "prayer." If God doesn't give these, the only reason can be we are not fit for them. Quite a mistake to think that God picks out a small aristocracy of virtue. I don't say He doesn't give more to some than to others, but He wants to make saints of us all. "Be ye perfect as your Father in Heaven is perfect."

✠ THE TRUTH ✠

BE quite sure that He wants every one of us to love Him very much. "Why I don't love Him more is because I don't belong to the select few." Quite wrong. "Why am I not nearer to God? Why don't I get as much help as others seem to get? I am a poor soul, and God has left me out, and I am to proceed at a jog-trot for the rest of my life."

It can't be true. He laid down His life for us. "He that spared not His own Son, how shall He not with Him also freely give us all things?" He Who became a little child for us can't be so unreasonable that if we hold our hands out He will say, "Oh no! these graces are kept for certain people." Supposing we start with a small stock, accept that grace, He'll give you

another.   No one has any right to say,
"For me sanctity is out of the question."
God is *delighted* to give any one of us
what we need.   The only thing He wants
to do — He has no greater pleasure — is
to give us His love.   We shouldn't approach Him in an indifferent way and say,
"If you have anything for me this morning, I am willing to take it, but I don't
care very much about it. . ."   You should
be greatly encouraged if you feel more and
more that you *want* God.

The more faithfully the obstacles are
being removed, the nearer you get to Him,
even as in approaching a fire you feel the
heat increase.   If any one can honestly
say, — I do feel I want God more than
ever before — I look back over twelve
months, and other interests seem to have
dwindled,   and   God's   interests   have
taken a larger part in my life — that is
excellent.   More independent of worldli-
ness, seeing His will more clearly and the
longing getting real — all excellent.

✠   "MY GOD"   ✠

"MY God, my God, why hast Thou for-
saken me?" Our Lord was in physical agony, and in great mental agony: in
that desolation of body and soul when we

should have expected His Father to come
to His help. He generally comes to the
aid of His saints in such circumstances.
Our Lord does not call Him "Father," but
"My God," as if God no longer loved or
cared for Him — a mystery, but no less
true. Solitude — or abandonment, with
some souls this trial recurs — this awful
wilderness. The nearer we get to God,
the more we feel there is no one but Him.
We must be severed from creatures if we
are to get near Him. This severance is
necessary if we are to get high in the
spiritual life. Only one Being we love
in the whole world — and that is God.

✠   HARD TO BEAR   ✠

EVERY one had abandoned our Lord.
God doesn't really forsake the soul,
but for our training and discipline seems
to. Our Lord prays, we ought to pray,
though it seems as if we were praying to
wood. Sometimes the darkness seems
peopled with horrors: our past sins con-
front us, everything we have been taught
seems a mockery. "Curse God and die."
That is the temptation to which we are ex-
posed. Is it tood hard to bear? Our Lord
says, "Very well, if you won't bear this
little thing for Me I must treat you as a

child, and give you milk." We must pray
to God, and He will certainly come to our
help. As He did to our Lord, "Father,
into Thy hands I commend my spirit."

The lesson for us is: If we want to love
Him we must make up our minds there is
no doubt about the suffering that will
come. When it comes, don't let us lose
heart, or think because we don't feel His
Presence He is not there. Or cry out too
soon, or think the trial is going to last
for ever. How else shall we get strong?
Don't we want to make some return to our
Lord? Surely we don't want a life without any trials or troubles? Let us make
ourselves very familiar with our Lord's
Passion. We get much nearer to Him
through faithfulness in times of stress and
difficulty than through sweetnesses and
consolations.

✠   SINCERE LOVE   ✠

"FATHER, forgive them, they know
not what they do." Our Lord kept
repeating these words—for His execution-
ers, the priests and others who had com-
passed His death. What wonderful love—
pleading for them. The reason—"For they
know not what they do." They did not
know He was God, but it was their own

fault. The prevailing sentiment with God
is one of extraordinary indulgence.   In
spite of all our sins, our Lord truly loves
us.   Throughout all we do there is that
element of ignorance and weakness which
enables Him to look pitifully on us and
love us.

Yet how many are saying, "He can't
love *me* quite sincerely.   He can't forget."
He makes such wonderful allowance for us
—we don't make enough ourselves.   Even
we, wretches though we be, if someone be-
haves very badly towards us, we entirely
forgive.   It passes out, not of our memory,
but of our hearts.   We shall never be on
proper terms with God till we believe in
His real love for us.   He, knowing how
difficult it is for us to be consistent and
good, forgives us so absolutely.   Don't
make the huge mistake of thinking it a
virtuous thing to feel you can't hope to be
in God's favor . . . you can't have too
strong a conviction of the infinite com-
passion of our Lord.

✠   TO EMMAUS   ✠

THE two disciples going to Emmaus are
encouraged to open their hearts to
Our Lord. He deliberately, of set purpose,
concealed from them who He was.   He

liked to listen to His praises from them,
and practised a loving deceit on them. The
disciples tell Him all that had happened
and all they had expected . . . "Those
were our hopes, and it is all gone. And
we, His followers, are all scattered, and
we don't know what to do. And there is
an extraordinary sequence to this matter.
Some women of our company say that
they have seen angels in the Tomb, and
the Body is not there, and we have been
in sore trouble ever since." Their hearts
were so full, they have let it all out.

✠   ENTHUSIASM   ✠

IT is a great gift of God to be capable
of a great enthusiasm. What are my
ways of looking at persons and things? Although these two men had given up all
hope, nothing would induce them to turn
against Him. It might have meant serious
trouble to them, but they were absolutely
loyal. We may have hopes, well-favored
hopes, and yet they seem dispelled. Although correct in the main fact, they were
wrong in the way they expected things to
come about. And we make exactly the
same mistake. We pray to God to help
us, and we are good enough to point out
to Him how it is to be done. Our way

is probably a very bad way. He says,
"Knock, and it shall be opened," but He
doesn't say *how*. We may be quite right
as to substance, but quite wrong as to
means to be used.

✠   PETTY NOTIONS   ✠

WHEN we pray for favors, I *hope* we
don't find fault with God. We are
very like spoilt children, and cry and think
we have good reason to sulk when things
go as we don't like. It may be God does
answer our prayers, and we don't know
it. You can't lean too heavily on the persuasion that God will help you, but not
that it is to be at such a time and in such
a way. Our Lord heard the disciples with
the greatest delight. "O foolish and slow
of heart," He began.

That is the matter with so many of us
—wanting to measure everything according to our own petty notions. If we had
only a little quickness of heart and trust
in God we should understand the Holy
Scriptures so much better. *"Ought not."*
Ought not I so to suffer? Unfortunately,
we so often go the other way. Suffering
and glory are inseparable. What a privilege to have heard the Inspirer of the
Scriptures explain them.

Meanwhile, it is near sundown. Our Lord makes as if He must push on. Another deceit on our Lord's part. Why did He pretend? In the language of love there are so many of these little devices. They constrained Him. You *must* stay and dine with us. As soon as He communicates them they know Him. Their hearts had burned within them — with love. So wonderful to hear His explanations. See, if you want to please our Lord, how much He likes us to speak of Him. Love Him want to do your best for Him. He doesn' mind our stupid mistakes, our involuntary faults. Be sure He will make our hearts burn within us.

✠   A NEEDED LESSON   ✠

THESE men's fears were by no means unfounded, but they are so full of our Lord, and the memory of His sufferings is so keen, they say it all out. Not a word in disparagement of Him. A lesson for us. As long as our Lord gives us bonbons, and every one says how good we are, all is well, and we think it a fine thing to be on our Lord's side; but when things go wrong it is a very different matter. They had had a stunning blow, and were dazed. Such a terrible catastrophe the world had never seen, nor will again. A young man cut off in the prime of life, under the eyes of His Mother, in such circumstances of pain and ignominy! They thought there was an end to all their hopes.

✠   "SLOW OF HEART"   ✠

MANY times we have thought we were going to get a solution to our difficulties, prayer getting easier, and then, all seems to go back again, and we say, "We thought at one time our Lord was going to give us this, and now——" At that very moment our Lord was walking with them! How truly He may say to us, Fools! Children! not to be able to understand what is as plain as the sun at noonday. We don't understand our Lord *has done* for us what we asked Him. Because our Lord does not grant our petition by the next post, He is not going to attend to us at all. "Oh, don't ask *me* to pray. God never answers *my* prayers."

What idiots we are! No one has ever yet said a real prayer and not received an answer from God. It is giving God the lie to talk such folly. It is not even necessary to be in a state of grace to get an answer to prayer. Further, God desires to answer our prayer much more than we

desire to make it. That kind of stupidity
God doesn't love. "Slow of heart," He
calls the disciples because they won't trust
in our Lord. We tap very gently, and
because the door is not at once opened, we
go away and think union with God refused us. . . Where has God said He will
only hear the prayers of holy people?
"Slow of heart" to believe God really does
want us to be saints. He says He does;
we say He doesn't: which is likely to be
right? If that sort of distrust is my habit
of mind, my prayer is no use: it is all
wrong. What our Lord wants is for us
to love Him. . . They ought to have un-
derstood that Christ *ought* so to have
suffered. We want virtue without trouble;
to be humble without humiliation, sympathy with Christ's sufferings without a
finger-ache ourselves.

☦   CONSTRAIN GOD   ☦

RECONSTRUCT your lives by the
light cast on them by these sayings of
our Lord. It has all been a huge mistake.
May you not say all those disappointments, all that apparent waste of energy,
those contradicting circumstances — all
are part of your discipline for eternity?
Ought not that to have been? . . . For-

given sin even may be a great help in the service of God. Your life has been as God permitted. There is no truth in talking of a life thrown away — marred — no truth in it. Besides, one minute's sorrow will undo it all, and make you at the present moment very dear to God. What ever has been, has been allowed to be, and will lead on to your eternal happiness. . .

They constrained Him. When our Lord seems to refuse us a favor, constrain Him. He can't hold out against the constraint of true love. Then He broke bread with them, and they knew Him, and He disappeared, "Did not our hearts burn within us . . . ?"

✠   PESSIMISTS   ✠

A GREAT hindrance to our spiritual advancement is the persuasion that for some reason or other God is not pleased with us. Most of us are pessimists in the spiritual life. We think "It would not be right for God to give me great graces; I have refused too many in the past." Such thoughts are the work of the Devil. God loves each one of us with such an intensity of love as it is impossible for us to conceive. He longs for our Communions, and misses us when we don't go. There is nothing God does while we are in the state of probation, the object of which is not to bring us to love Him. He allows trials to come upon us for our greater perfection. It should be a source of great comfort to us to know that the circumstances in which we are placed are just those circumstances in which, out of the whole world, we can serve God best.

Do not be afraid of presumption. He says: "My arms are open; come near to Me."

✠ SMALL GRACES ✠

ALWAYS listen to the promptings of grace. When we hear an uncharitable criticism we often long to say: "I entirely agree with you." Remain silent. These small graces mount up and up. Our Lord says: "The first and greatest command- ment is, Thou shalt love the Lord thy God, with thy whole heart, and with thy whole soul, and with thy whole mind, and with thy whole strength." (Matt. xxii. 38; Mark xii. 30.) Is it for us to throw doubt on God's word? God intends us all to serve Him out of love.

When God wants a soul to come near Him He gives the invitation. He begins

by giving the soul a desire to know Him,
to love Him. If any one feels that desire,
no matter how feebly, be assured it comes
from God. He does not begin and leave
His work unfinished. He will gratify the
desire which He Himself has inspired, if
we will but be faithful. Were He never
to gratify us He would be acting like a
mother who held a picture in front of her
child, and whenever the child reached out
for it, drew the picture away, merely teas-
ing the child.

✠   TIME TO BEGIN   ✠

DON'T say "All these years I have not
served Him well; how can I now suddenly begin?" Time is nothing with God.
Say rather, "He who has begun the good
work in me will perfect it" (Phil. i. 6.)
Let us say to our Lord "It is Thou Thy-
self, Lord who has made me want to love
Thee. Do Thou Who hast filled me with
this desire give me greater love."

Many difficulties in the spiritual life are
really created by ourselves. We worry
and hurry and seem almost to think it a
virtue to be impatient with ourselves. The
best way to get something from God is
certainly not to worry. Take things
quietly: don't rush. The saints did not

become perfect in a day; it took them a long time to mould their characters on the Divine pattern, and what work is so wearisome as work on our character! Yet they were not impatient; they were amazingly cheerful. They never said, "There's no chance of my ever getting over this," as we are tempted to. They knew better. Why is there no chance? Doesn't God love me infinitely? For improvement in the spiritual life we want a never-failing cheerfulness and courage.

✠   "SERVE ME"   ✠

OUR Lord says: "Don't worry; leave it to Me; serve Me; I will take care of you." Isn't it a pity you fritter and waste your time and strength. If a thing is to be regretted, regret it; then put it away. Our poor little petty intellects and wills won't bear dividing. What a pity not to live in the present; a tranquil sorrow for the past, good; but no anxious retrospection or anticipation.

Would it please you if your children were always doubting whether you were going to love them to-morrow?

The saints of God lived in the present; they did their best, and left it to God.

Take the cup of humiliations and drain

it, and every sun that rises and every sun
that sets shall witness a glorious life. We
can't help feeling the pain of humiliations;
we can't help feeling beaten and bruised
and broken all over. That does not matter; what matters is that we harbor no
bitterness, cherish no resentment.

☩   REACHING HIM   ☩

PEOPLE told falsehoods about our
Lord, said that dreadful thing about
His casting out devils through Beelzebub.
These things wounded the tender Heart of
Jesus, but He bore them patiently, without bitterness, without resentment, gladly
for my sake. Remembering this, let me
say to Him: "Dear Lord, when You find
that I am very cowardly, very impatient,
and I say 'I can't bear this; I can't endure
that'; don't take me at my word; give me
strength to bear and to endure; make me
understand You better and love You
better and love You more."

It is a horrible doctrine to say that God
does not want to speak to *your* soul.
Prayer consists in getting into communi-
cation with God in some sort of way. The
way does not matter in the least, and the
easier the better. If only you are in
earnest, you will reach Him, for He is

yearning to give Himself to you. Do not
sigh and say: "If God would only show
Himself to me!" He will; He wants to;
He will let you touch Him, feel Him, taste
Him.

Is it the pure love of God that makes
you anxious about your prayer? Or is it
only the desire to be saved trouble? Or,
I have a faint, far-off suspicion, has it
something to do with humility? Why can
others pray with such facility and not I?
Leave others alone and you will soon
learn to pray.

✠   **BASELESS FEAR**   ✠

SOME people's one preoccupation—ob-
session we might call it—seems to be
the fear that there is something they have
forgotten and which God will spring upon
them at their judgment. Where do these
terrors come from? This contradiction of
the heart? This distrust in God's goodness? St. John says: "Perfect love casteth
out fear." (1 John iv. 18). And our Lord
used to say: "It is I; *be not afraid*." (John
vi. 20.)

Religion is not a question of perpetually
avoiding something. Yet there are those
who seem to think the essence of the
spiritual life consists in examining their

conscience, always thinking of their past, and having a catalogue of their sins ever before them. They take the last gleams of hope out of their unhappy souls and make of their spiritual life a perpetual shuddering. But our Lord was gentle with His Apostles, and they with all their faults were never uncomfortable with Him. To avoid sin, do good.

✠ A FULL HEART ✠

GOD judges us not so much by details as by the whole, the purpose of our life. To be drifting, to have no settled aim in life, is unsatisfactory for everyone: working nothing out, ending in nothing. Everyone ought to be living, working, for something. What are you at?

The nearer a soul gets to God, the more it loves to dwell on our Lord's Human Nature.

Like a sponge plunged into the ocean, so must you lose yourself in the Sacred Heart of Jesus, that the waters of love may surround and deluge your soul on every side.

The love of God can *fill* your heart.

CPSIA information can be obtained at www.ICGtesting.com
Printed in the USA
BVOW07*1243040115

381747BV00003B/17/P